Little George 2

Created by C Edgar Humphrey, MFA

Illustrated by Jonathan Jacobo Raygoza

Editorial Design by Karly Gonzalez and Luis Gongora

Administrator Enoc Rodriguez

Acknowledgements:

There are vivid memories of mentors, heroes, and supportive influential people… and pets.

MISSY – My first long-term relationship; lasted thirteen years. RIP little puppy friend. She slept under my covers, and sometimes with her head on my pillow. She loved going fishing with me, and scratching up flat rocks from underwater at the pond… a true rock hound. (Sorry)

CHICKEN LITTLE – She learned to jump back and forth over a stick (thank you Charles Pavarini), for pieces of bread. She was being groomed to be a star. She spent her nights in my plant room, perched in the Pittosporum bush.

FRED - A baby peacock I raised, who grew to spectacular manhood at the gentleman 'farm'. He guarded my house nightly, sitting on the roof, warning anything that walked by (2 legs or 4 legs), to get the HECK out! (Hallllpppppp!) (What a tail!)

FISH IN WELL-LIT AQUARIA – Their never-closing eyes watched over my nights, scaring away boogilee things lurking under my bed. I feel sure they prevented nightly kidnappings.

WHAT A CORPS! Praise be, to our loving and loyal pets. (Of course I fed them well).

There is some "Little George" in all of us. There certainly was some in me... and still, a few leftovers.

CEH

Little George 2

Little George

He's good, He's bad, and often care-less.

He hates sitting in classes at school; loves to play and make mud tortillas.

He's just a normal kid... usually.

Little Geroge sometimes thinks he's weird because he bakes a cake but can't follow the recipe. He can carry on a conversation with his favorite dog... well, who can't?

George tolerates adults, but likes his friends, animals and daydreams better.

Someday "Little George" will be "Big George". How unexciting!

(He didn't do his Homework)

(He sticks his homework in his backpack
before his mom can check it)

(He goes into the bathroom)

(George brushes his teeth for 2 minutes)

(George cleans his ears and
face with a wash cloth)

(George is as clean as a whistle)

(George turns bright red because he got caught.)

(He says, trying to think of something)

(His mom says, knowing he will make up a story)

Your teacher, Ms. Webber, will be mad!

(George climbs into bed like a little old man)

(In the black room, he hears something
scratching by his bed. He is terribly scared)

(Suddendly a giant monster
pops up by his bed)

(The monster becomes a spider, with
a teacher wig, big glasses and combat boots)

(She spins a cocoon around him)

(She sticks his unfinished homework through a hole in the cocoon)

(George has a tantrum!)

(George gives up and does his Math)

(He hands it out of the cocoon)

(She opens a slit in the cocoon and lets George out)

(George climbs into bed and puts the Math on his pillow next to his head)

(The alarm goes off at 7AM)

(George opens one eye)

(He looks very surprised)

(George says in a whisper)

(She pats him on his head)

(Little George smiles and looks at his pet spider in the lampshade)

Do your math before you go to bed,
and your teacher will be very happy.

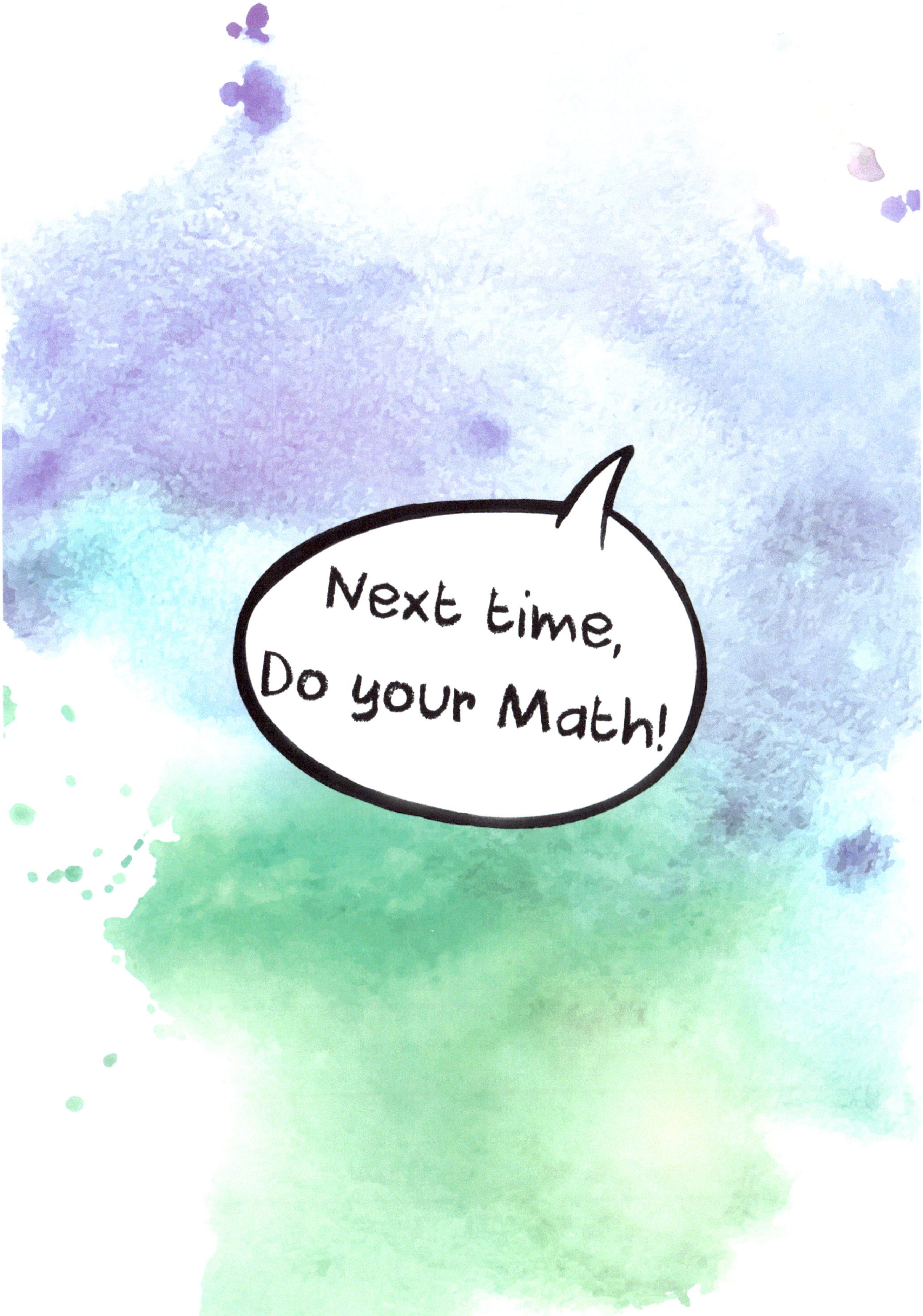
Next time,
Do your Math!